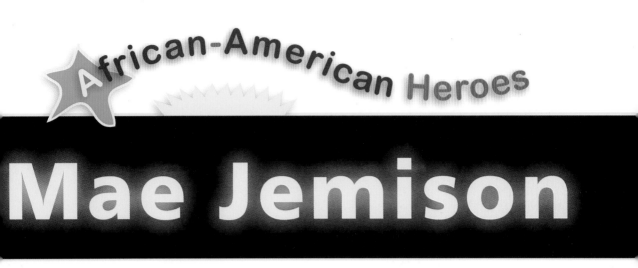

African-American Heroes

Mae Jemison

Stephen Feinstein

Enslow Elementary
an imprint of

 Enslow Publishers, Inc.
40 Industrial Road
Box 398
Berkeley Heights, NJ 07922
USA

http://www.enslow.com

Words to Know

astronaut—A person who goes into space.

engineering—The study of how things work.

gravity—A force that pulls things toward bigger things. Earth's gravity pulls things toward the ground.

NASA—National Aeronautics and Space Administration. The organization in charge of the U.S. space program.

Peace Corps (CORE)—A group of Americans who go all over the world to help other people.

space shuttle—A spaceship that moves people and things between Earth and space.

volunteer—To help other people without pay.

Enslow Elementary, an imprint of Enslow Publishers, Inc.

Enslow Elementary® is a registered trademark of Enslow Publishers, Inc.

Library of Congress Cataloging-in-Publication Data

Feinstein, Stephen.
    Mae Jemison / Stephen Feinstein.
        p. cm. — (African-American heroes)
    Includes index.
    ISBN-13: 978-0-7660-2762-6
    ISBN-10: 0-7660-2762-7
    1. Jemison, Mae, 1956–   —Juvenile literature. 2. African American women astronauts—Biography—Juvenile literature. 3. Astronauts—United States—Biography—Juvenile literature. I. Title.
    TL789.85.J46F45 2006
    629.450092—dc22
    [B]   2006026900

Printed in the United States of America

10 9 8 7 6 5 4 3 2 1

To Our Readers: We have done our best to make sure all Internet Addresses in this book were active and appropriate when we went to press. However, the author and the publisher have no control over and assume no liability for the material available on those Internet sites or on links to other Web sites. Any comments or suggestions can be sent by e-mail to comments@enslow.com or to the address on the back cover.

Illustration Credits: AP/Wide World, pp. 15, 16; Getty Images, pp. 2, 20; courtesy of the National Aeronautics and Space Administration, pp. 1, 3, 5, 8, 9, 10, 11, 14, 16, 17, 18, 19, 21; courtesy of the Peace Corps, p. 13; Photodisc, p. 6; Shutterstock.com, pp. 3, 7, 9.

Cover Illustration: Courtesy of the National Aeronautics and Space Administration.

Contents

Chapter 1
Serious About Science

Mae Jemison was born on October 17, 1956, in Alabama. When she was four, her family moved to Chicago, Illinois.

Mae's mother, Dorothy, was a teacher. She and Mae's father, Charles, made sure that their children did well in school.

Ever since she was a little girl, Mae wanted to become a scientist. Her teacher said, "You mean you want to become a nurse." But Mae knew what she wanted.

In the first grade, she wanted to do a science project. She helped her big sister, Ada Sue, and her big brother, Ricky, with their science projects.

Mae Jemison was the first African-American woman in space. Here she is shown floating without gravity.

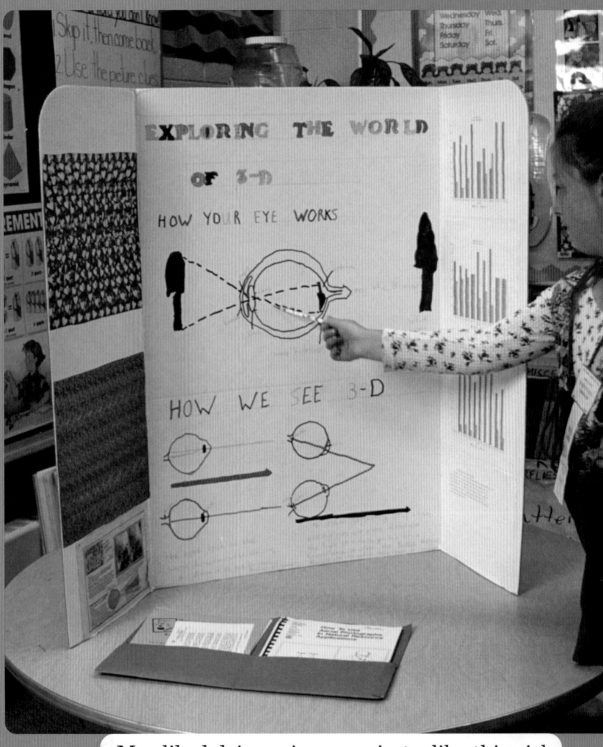

Mae liked doing science projects, like this girl.

When Mae was in the third grade, she got a science project of her own to do. It was all about how life on Earth started and how it changed over time. Mae worked on her science project all the way up to the sixth grade.

Mae wanted to understand the world. She read about the dinosaurs. She found out about all kinds of early plant and animal life. She also read about the stars and the planets. She often went to the library and stayed there until it closed. On the way home, she would look up at the stars twinkling in the sky. She wondered where they came from.

Mae liked to read about dinosaurs and early life on Earth.

Chapter 2

Mae Dreams About Becoming an Astronaut

In addition to books about science, Mae loved to read made-up stories. She read about people who traveled in space to other planets. She read about strange worlds far away. Mae dreamed that someday she would go into space.

Like this girl, Mae liked to look at the stars.

On July 20, 1969, **astronauts** Neil Armstrong, Buzz Aldrin, and Mike Collins

became the first people to go to the moon. Mae was very excited. She read all about the moon landing. If only there were some way that she could become an astronaut too.

The astronauts even left footprints on the moon!

But Mae saw that all the astronauts were white men. Would NASA—the National Aeronautics and Space Administration—ever choose an African-American woman to become an astronaut?

Buzz Aldrin stands next to the American flag the astronauts put on the moon.

Apollo 11 blasting off to the moon.

Chapter 3

Mae Becomes a Doctor

Mae studied chemistry and **engineering** in college. She graduated in 1977. Then Mae decided she wanted to be a doctor to help other people. So she went to medical school.

While studying to be a doctor, Mae did **volunteer** work in Africa and Asia. She took care of people in small villages.

In 1981, Mae became a doctor. First she worked in Los Angeles, California. The next year she went back to Africa as a doctor in the **Peace Corps**. She helped people in Africa for several years. Then in 1985, Mae moved back to California.

This Peace Corps volunteer (on right) went to Ghana, in Africa.

Chapter 4 Mae's Dream Comes True

While working as a doctor, Mae took more classes in engineering. She enjoyed her work. But she still dreamed about space travel.

One day in 1985, Mae learned that NASA was looking for new people to become astronauts.

Mae decided to try. Perhaps she now had a chance to be chosen. African-American men had already been in the space program. And in 1983, Sally Ride had become the first American woman to go into space.

Sally Ride was the first American woman in space.

On January 28, 1986, the **space shuttle** *Challenger* blew up and crashed shortly after it took off. All the astronauts aboard were killed. Mae knew that going into space was dangerous. But she was not afraid. In February 1987, NASA chose Mae for the astronaut program.

The space shuttle *Challenger* exploded just after liftoff. Even though she knew it was dangerous, Mae still wanted to go into space.

Mae had to learn many things before she could be an astronaut.

Mae lived and worked at the Johnson Space Center in Houston, Texas, for five years. While training to be an astronaut, she learned all about the space shuttle. She studied many different science subjects.

On September 12, 1992, Mae blasted into space aboard the *Endeavour*. She was the first African-American woman in space. During her eight days in space, Mae did science experiments. She wanted to learn how to keep people healthy in space.

The crew of the *Endeavour* posed for a photo in space.

Mae did many experiments in space.

After going into space, Mae went all over the world to tell people about it.

After she returned to Earth, Mae had a new dream. She wanted to use science to make the world a better place. Mae left NASA in 1993 and started her own company.

To share her ideas, Mae taught science in college and gave speeches all around the country. She always told young people not to be afraid to follow their dreams.

Mae's Own Words

"The thing that I have done throughout my life is to do the best job that I can and to be me."

Timeline

1956—Mae is born in Alabama on October 17.

1977—Mae graduates from Stanford University with a science degree.

1981—Mae gets a medical degree from Cornell University Medical College.

1982—Mae joins the Peace Corps in Africa.

1987—Mae is accepted into NASA's astronaut program.

1992—On September 12, Mae becomes the first African-American woman to go into space.

1993—Mae retires from NASA.

1994—Mae starts a company to take technology to other countries and to improve science education.

Learn More

Books

Braun, Eric. *Mae Jemison*. Mankato, Minn.: Capstone Press, 2006.

Murphy, Patricia J. *Exploring Space With an Astronaut*. Berkeley Heights, N.J.: Enslow Publishers, Inc., 2004.

Striessguth, Tom. *Mae Jemison*. Mankato, Minn.: Bridgestone Books, 2003.

Web Sites

Amazing Space
<http://amazing-space.stsci.edu>

NASA Kids' Club
<http://www.nasa.gov>
Click on "For Students," then click on "Grades K-4."

Index